# PLAYING WITH
# SURFACE DESIGN

COURTNEY CERRUTI
WITH PHOTOGRAPHY BY LIZ DALY

## MODERN TECHNIQUES FOR PAINTING, STAMPING, PRINTING, AND MORE

 **Quarry Books**
100 Cummings Center, Suite 406L
Beverly, MA 01915

quarrybooks.com • www.craftside.net

First published in the United States of America by
Quarry Books, a member of
Quarto Publishing Group USA Inc.
100 Cummings Center
Suite 406-L
Beverly, Massachusetts 01915-6101
Telephone: (978) 282-9590
Fax: (978) 283-2742
www.quarrybooks.com
Visit www.craftside.net for a behind-the-scenes peek at our crafty world!

Library of Congress Cataloging-in-Publication Data available

ISBN: 978-1-63159-036-8

Digital edition published in 2015
eISBN: 978-1-62788-343-6

10 9 8 7 6 5 4 3 2 1

Design: Landers Miller Design
Layout: Megan Jones Design
Photography: Liz Daly, cover & pages 1—116; gallery images, courtesy of contributors

Printed in China

FOR ALL MY STUDENTS—
THANK YOU FOR INSPIRING ME AND MOVING ME FORWARD
IN MY PRACTICE OF MAKING AND TEACHING ART.

# CONTENTS

# INTRODUCTION

Some of the techniques in this book are quick and simple ways to create marks and patterns. Others are more involved printing methods that will yield a variety of results. The more elaborate processes of gelatin monoprinting and making paste paper are explained in the process chapter, while methods such as marbling and stamping are described within the projects. This book is meant to introduce surface design into your everyday practice through projects that are beautiful and attainable. Don't be afraid to combine methods for even greater exploration and cross-pollination.

While writing this book I thought long and hard about what it means to categorize something as surface design. An easy answer is to say that surface design is any image, pattern, graphic, or mark made on a given surface—and that's true. Often there are connotations that surface design is limited to commercial products, textiles, or dishware, but I think that's really changing. Most methods of creating designs rely on a computer, either in creating the imagery itself or in making a pattern from existing imagery for printing or use. With sites such as Society6 and Spoonflower, untrained artists and doodlers can put their work on T-shirts and phone cases, or even on fabric and paper—and that's awesome.

*Playing with Surface Design* is about delving into methods rooted in traditional printmaking and painting techniques, but executed with a modern interpretation. Just like any other medium or artistic practice, these are the methods developed over a decade of playing, discovery, failure, and success. These are the methods that *I* love and use, and they should be the foundation for your own discovery and play.

*Playing with Surface Design* is a book to help you make patterns and designs that are fluid, intentional, and impactful—without a lot of fuss. The methods allow you to explore various mediums, both traditional and new, as well as play with the simple act of making marks on a page. Dip your brush into a pot of paint and create patterned paper, comb through tinted paste for faux bois, or stamp on linen for quick and easy home décor. Forget what you know about using paint and ink, and be ready to dive in with the enthusiasm of your five-year-old self. Accept that paste paper is the new finger painting, and don't be afraid to let yourself play.

# GETTING STARTED:
## materials and processes

# MONOPRINTING: GELATIN

Monoprints are prints that are unique in their creation. Impressions or prints are made one at a time and often include more painterly methods of image making than other types of printmaking. You can make a print from almost any surface, creating an image by painting, rolling ink over collages, or creating textures and impressions on the surface of a printing plate. Once you've created a painted or inked image, you press paper to the printing surface and pull a print.

There are many ways to make monoprints. My favorite way is using gelatin because the effect is unmistakable. Rolling ink on the slick surface of a slab of gelatin, laying objects into the wet paint, and pulling a print is magic every time. The unexpected beauty in every print incites an insatiable curiosity that can only be cured by an afternoon of printing.

# WHY USE GELATIN?

What I love about gelatin is that the plate stays moist throughout the entire printing process. The effect leaves you with a print that is more watercolor-like than any other method. It is hard to reproduce that painterly effect using other materials. You can use a similar process to pull prints from a silicone plate, such as a Gelli plate, but it will result in bolder prints. The printing methods in this book will work well on other surfaces (including a Gelli plate), but I urge you to try the gelatin at least once. It is simply unexpected and beautiful, and how often can you use Jell-O as an art material?

# TYPES OF PRINTING MATERIALS

Botanicals are ideal for creating texture and imagery. Vines, leaves, petals, and ferns can be combined to create images that are both bold and graphic or soft and feathery, depending on how you print them. Look for plant life that is fresh and flexible and without thorns or sharp edges. Chunky, woody, or dried items can gouge the surface of the gelatin, causing skips and unprinted spots on your final prints.

### FIBERS, FEATHERS, AND FABRIC

String, yarn, and ropes can create fluid, organic lines as well as delicate details and texture. Fabrics with open or large weaves work well for creating texture and pattern. Feathers make a lovely print! As you print, a feather will change its shape and texture from the ink, giving you varying results every time.

### FOAM, PLASTIC, AND PAPER SHAPES

You can create your own shapes using cardstock or craft foam. Take a walk down the kids' aisle of your local craft store and you'll find dozens of geometric shapes and objects made from brightly colored foam. These foam shapes are an easy way to create graphic lines and patterns. You can also cut paper to create shapes that will leave a negative space in the printing. Do be careful when cutting sharp shapes in cardstock as they can dig into the gelatin surface.

You can also find textured sheets of foam in the kids' crafting aisle. These sheets can be pressed onto the inked gelatin to create an even pattern of lines, dots, squiggles, and more. In addition to craft supplies, check out garage sales or dollar stores for plastic doilies, place mats, and other interesting textures.

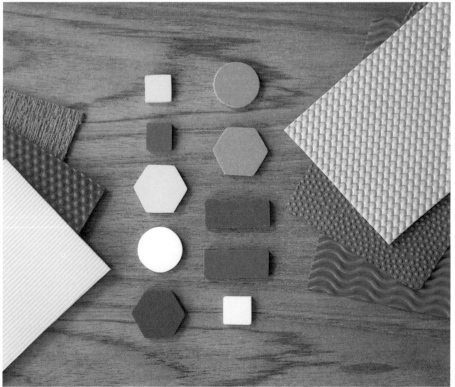

# PAPERS

Gelatin prints are easy and quick to make, and you can use most papers to pull a good-looking print. Using hot-press watercolor papers and printmaking papers will give you clean, saturated images. Using textured papers will result in more textured prints. You can also use copy paper to pull a print. The heavy-bodied papers will usually behave better and lie flat, but you can also weight prints made on inexpensive papers that tend to curl under a heavy stack of books once the prints are dry.

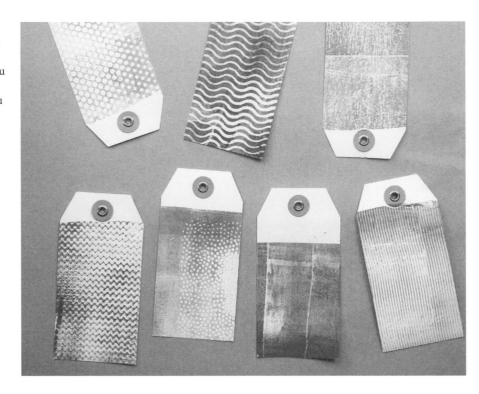

# INKS

Water-based printing inks are ideal for printing on gelatin. Printing inks are heavier bodied than acrylic paints. They roll out nicely (the sound of rolling ink is amazing!) and give an even, consistent, saturated layer of color. Best of all, printing inks clean up easily with water. You might be tempted to use acrylic paints, but they are hard to roll evenly and apply to the gelatin surface. Gelatin creates a soft, slippery surface that results in watercoloresque prints. The combination of the wet surface of the gelatin and the thick ink will result in a soft layer

of color. You can buy water-based printing inks in tubes or in pots. If you're using inks in pots, an old credit card or palette knife is handy for applying ink.

Even though your printing surface might only be 9 x 12 inches (23 x 30.5 cm) you can still make larger prints. It's helpful if the gelatin comes close to the top of your container to avoid crumpling your paper while printing. Don't be afraid to try printing larger papers on a smaller printing surface.

# PRINTING ON GELATIN

## MATERIALS

**Unflavored gelatin:** I use Knox brand. You'll need four packets for each printing plate.

**Cookie sheet or 9 x 12-inch (23 x 30.5 cm) baking dish:** It is important to use a clean sheet without any residue.

**Water-based printing inks:** Start with a light, medium, and dark color to test various printing techniques. Yellow, red, and blue are good choices, and the addition of black makes for high-contrast, dramatic prints.

**Brayers:** One dedicated for each color of ink.

**Nonporous surface for rolling up inks:** I use a rigid sheet of acrylic, but you could also use a clean cookie sheet, a metal counter, or a thick plate of glass.

**Flat, textural objects for creating prints and patterns:** Items such as paper doilies, dollar-store lace place mats, leaves, yarn, twine, feathers, petals, and cut paper shapes work well. Avoid items that have sharp, thick edges as they will cut into the gelatin and degrade the printing surface rapidly.

*Create patterned pages from colored office bond paper to use in collage and other mixed-media work.*

## STEP 1 MAKE GELATIN PRINTING PLATE

For an average-size cookie sheet, make a batch of unflavored, color-free gelatin using four (2½ teaspoons, or 7 g) packets. Read the manufacturer's directions on how to make the gelatin; it's usually a ratio of one packet of gelatin to 2 cups (470 ml) of water.

Pour the gelatin into the cookie sheet or baking dish, and transfer to the fridge. If the lip of your cookie sheet is shallow or the gelatin is very close to the rim of your dish, place the empty sheet into the refrigerator FIRST, then pour in the gelatin. I've dumped entire trays of gelatin into the back of the fridge and onto the floor!

When stirring or pouring the gelatin, if you create a lot of bubbles, use a plain sheet of copy paper and gently drag it across the surface to pull the bubbles to the edge of the tray. Allow the gelatin to harden for about an hour—then it's ready to use for printing.

## STEP 2 SET UP YOUR PRINTING AREA

Squeeze a 3-inch (7.6 cm) line of ink onto your ink-rolling station. You can mix colors directly on your inking surface. Using a credit card, mix colors by working the ink back and forth, scooping it up and squeegeeing across in a 3-inch (7.6 cm) line until the colors are thoroughly mixed. You can repeat this for all the colors you plan to print with, or use the colors straight out of the tube as is. If your printing surface only allows for you to roll up one color at a time, start with the lightest color, then clean up using your credit card, water, and a paper towel.

Once all your colors are laid out, you'll want to spread the ink evenly for printing. Using your brayer, roll the ink down from your 3-inch (7.6 cm) line. It feels natural to just roll the brayer back and forth, but you actually want to pick the brayer up and let it spin every time you get to the bottom of the line of ink you just pulled. This will allow the ink to distribute evenly.

*Roll ink until it makes a solid band before painting.*

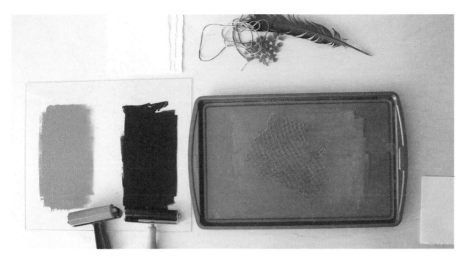

*Place netting or other flat object onto inked surface.*

*Press paper gently over object.*

*Image of mailing tags of first and second prints.*

### STEP 3  APPLY INK TO GELATIN

Once your brayer is nicely inked, roll a layer of ink onto the gelatin surface. I usually start with my lightest color and print dozens of pages in the first color. Roll the brayer back and forth until you see color appear on the tray. The ink will not be as saturated on the gelatin as it is on the ink surface. Sometimes you'll need to make several passes with the brayer to get a good coat of ink, especially if you're using the gelatin plate for the first time.

### STEP 4  PLACE OBJECTS

This is the fun part—now you get to compose your image! Using the materials you've gathered, place the objects onto the gelatin plate. Lightly place objects onto the surface of the gelatin. You don't need to press them; you'll do that when you pull the print. Once you place something down, don't lift it up again because it's already made an impression in the ink. Start with smaller, textured, or overall patterns initially. Doilies, fabric, or nets (the ones oranges or onions are packaged in) work well for this initial layer.

### STEP 5  PULL FIRST AND SECOND PRINTS

With all your objects in place, carefully lay a sheet of paper. Gently press the entire paper, being careful to press around all your objects. The larger the objects, the more space there is between the paper and the inked surface; this gap will leave white spaces that won't print if you don't press evenly. Thoroughly press the paper so you get a clean and clear impression. Carefully pull back your paper to reveal your first print!

The first print will be bold and bright with negative space where your objects were. Carefully remove the objects and pull your second print with a fresh sheet of paper, again making sure to press lightly. The second print will be soft and full of subtle texture. Second prints often look like fossils, especially when working with botanicals.

After every pulling of a print you'll need to re-ink the surface of your gelatin.

It works best to pull numerous prints in this first color run. Go ahead and print, re-inking after your first and second printing, until you've used up all of your rolled ink or when you're ready to play with a new color. You'll notice that pulling a print also cleans the surface of the gelatin. If you're working with paper that is smaller than your plate, you can use extra sheets of paper to pull up the additional color that was left behind.

Use a single sheet of paper to pull up all the unused ink, placing paper in sections over the surface of the gelatin until all of the ink is removed. I love the way these pages create edges, stripes, or little vignette frames on a page that can be used for additional printing, collage, or even as a matte to frame a photograph.

## STEP 6 SWITCHING COLORS

To switch ink colors, simply roll out a new color on the gelatin. If you are using a small ink-rolling surface, you can change out your colors by cleaning the ink up with water and a paper towel. Rinse and dry your brayer thoroughly before rolling up a new color.

For the second pass at printing, switch to a new color ink. Repeat pulling first and second prints with this new color, printing on top of all the pages you printed in the first print run. The more contrast you have between print runs, the bolder your prints will be. Prints that are too soft and feathery can be livened by using printing objects that have beautiful and large shapes (such as leaves). Pump up the contrast even further by printing a final layer with an indigo or black ink.

You can do any number of print runs, switching colors each time. I often will do one or two colors and then if I'm still needing more punch, finish with a darker layer of ink for the final print run.

After a while your gelatin surface will start to degrade. This will happen sooner if you use sharp or rigid objects that cut into the surface of your gelatin. Any place you get a cut or mar will result in an uninked and, therefore, unprinted space in your final print; I call these "skips." Eventually, little

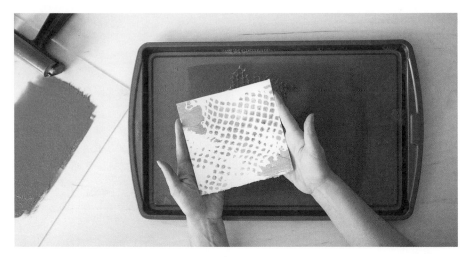

*Pull your first print to reveal bold, negative shapes and patterns.*

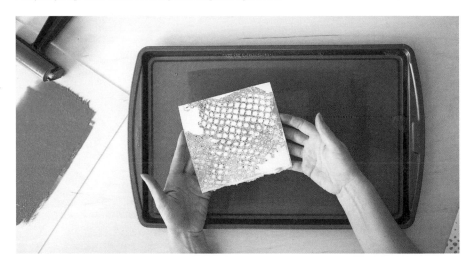

*Using the same objects to print from over and over will result in ink buildup over time. The darker ink in this print is residue from a previous print session. These unexpected colors and textures can create dimension and depth in your work.*

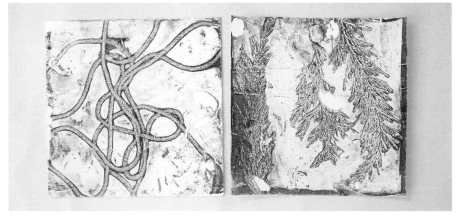

*A second pull results in a softer, more detailed print that can resemble a fossil or a botanical rubbing.*

*Playing with objects and printed layers will result in prints that range from soft and dreamy to bold and dramatic.*

chunks of gelatin may start to pull up as you roll ink. You can keep printing away and be creative with your composition and layering prints. The great thing about this happening is now you can be even more experimental and adventurous. Feel free to start layering on heavy or even spiky objects to see how they'll print—things such as keys, bike gears, chain, or thick plants can make really awesome images and now is the time to use them!

## STEP 7  CLEAN UP

Thoroughly clean the brayers with water and allow them to dry before storing them. Excess ink on the printing surface can be scraped up with a credit card and any residue washed away with water and a paper towel. Sometimes you can pull the slab of gelatin out from its container in one motion. Feel free to use your fingers and really dig into the gelatin and scoop it out (this will really delight your inner child!).

The nature of this printing process uses very little ink—your prints will be dry almost immediately after they are pulled. You can stack prints and weight them after your print session if any of your pages are warped or curled.

## TROUBLESHOOTING

If ink isn't sticking to gelatin when working on a fresh plate or a plate you've been using for a while, lightly wet the surface of the gelatin using a spray bottle, and then pull a blank print, without ink, to refresh the plate. You can use a spray bottle of water to lightly wet the surface and pull a clean print to refresh the plate. The rolled ink may start to dry on the ink-rolling surface. If you already have an ample amount of ink, then refresh what you have with a light spray of water. Incorporate the ink and water by rerolling the brayer, and then try re-inking the surface of the gelatin plate.

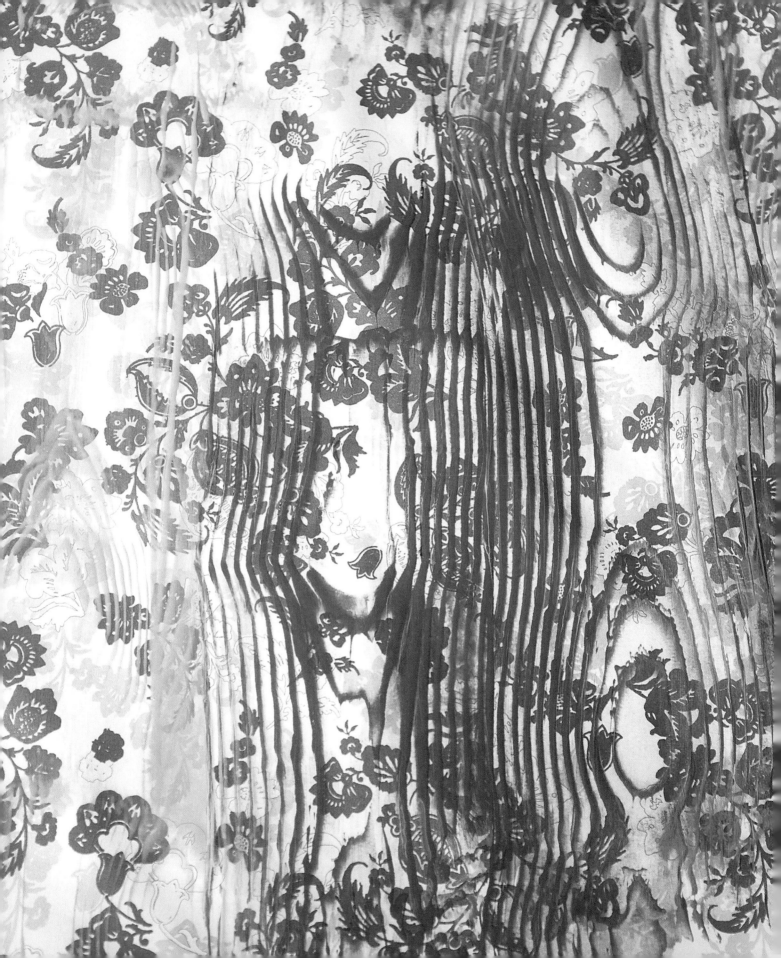

# PASTE PAPER

Paste paper is a traditional way of making patterned papers using paste and pigment. Various combs and mark-making tools are dragged across the surface of the paper to create geometric patterns. Most often paste papers are monochromatic or have a simple two-color pattern. Paste paper has been a popular choice as end papers in books in Europe and the United States for hundreds of years. More recently, artists and craftsmen have adopted paste papers for other applications in book and paper arts, including cover design, collage, and other mixed-media work. Eric Carle, the author of the iconic *The Very Hungry Caterpillar*, creates beautiful paste papers. He then uses the hand-painted papers to collage images for his children's book illustrations.

I love this technique. It's like finger painting for adults. But, my approach to paste paper is a little different. I enjoy pushing the traditional method by using a wood-graining tool to create faux-bois prints. I also use modern color palettes. I've been known to throw in a neon paint or even a metallic gold just to mix things up a little!

Paste paper is one of those techniques that appears super simple—which it is—but requires a bit of practice to master. Here are a few tips to get you started.

High-contrast color combinations between paper and paint yield the most eye-catching results. Some of my favorites are red paint on aqua paper, metallic gold paint on white or aqua paper, and black paint on curry yellow paper.

As your prints dry the colors will shift slightly. Often colors will look vibrant and dark when wet, then fade to a softer shade once dry. Keep this in mind when mixing paints and creating patterns.

DON'T oversaturate your paper with methyl cellulose and paint. DO get even coverage over the entire surface of the paper. If you glob on the methyl cellulose and paint, you'll get thick, runny patterns instead of clean lines, and your papers will take forever to dry.

Give yourself permission to play! Experiment with color combinations and mark making. If you don't like something when you make it, keep going. Come back to a piece once it's dry. You'll often be surprised by how much you like it later.

The amazing thing about paste paper is that even the smallest scrap can look like a painting. Punching out circles or cutting strips from a larger sheet you didn't like might yield small pieces you love.

A boring or unsatisfying pattern can also make a great base for a second printing. Once a piece is dry, cover it with methyl cellulose and a dark paint and make a new pattern on top. My go-to for this rescue process is what I call "wood-grain plaid." I'll slap some black or gold paint straight from the bottle onto a patterned dry piece that's been primed with a fresh layer of methyl cellulose. Using a wood-graining tool, I comb through to yield a bold "plaid" print—works every time.

## MATERIALS

**Methyl cellulose:** A low-tack, reversible, and archival glue made from plant cellulose. It comes in powder form and is mixed with water to create a gel-like substance. You'll only need a few tablespoons of the powder to mix up a large batch of gel for printing. Once mixed, it can last up to several weeks if stored in a clean, airtight container in a cabinet or in the fridge.

For our purposes, methyl cellulose will act as a lubricant and medium during the printing process. It dries clear with a matte finish. You can find methyl cellulose online at Tallas and other bookbinding suppliers, or even at some Paper Source stores (see Resources, page 143).

**Acrylic craft paint or powdered pigments:** Experiment with what you have on hand. Inexpensive craft acrylics may work great, but as you begin to play with pastel colors things can get muddy quickly. Paints with a higher concentration of pigments such as Golden Fluid Acrylics will yield brighter, bolder patterns.

I love using metallic in my papers. My favorite gold paint is Emperor's Gold by DecoArt; you can find it at most craft supply stores. I use metallic and black paint straight out of the bottle because methyl cellulose tends to dull and dilute the colors.

**Low, wide cups:** Muffin tins or plastic yogurt containers are perfect for mixing paints. Wide-mouth class jars work well, too. Unused paint may be saved for a week or so if well sealed and stored in a dark, cool area.

**Foam brushes:** One dedicated brush for every color you mix, plus one for clear methyl cellulose, one for black, and one for gold paint. Mixing brushes creates muddy colors. Avoid washing brushes while printing because you will introduce water into the process. Foam brushes give smooth, even coverage, but they absorb paint quickly. Keep them propped on top of your jars or off to the side when printing. Don't leave them sitting in the paint containers.

**Popsicle sticks or plastic knives:** Essential for stirring methyl cellulose and paint. Don't use your foam brushes to mix paint.

**Baby wipes or wet paper towels:** Use these for cleaning tools in between printings.

**Variety of papers:** If you plan on using your paste paper for gift wrapping or bookbinding, use a medium-weight paper that can bend and fold easily once painted. A 60 lb (89 gsm) paper is a good weight; Paper Source sells a variety of lovely colors that are perfect for paste paper. You can also paint thicker papers, such as cardstock, to create shapes for layering or card making.

Thinner papers such as bond or copy paper tend to wrinkle and warp, while thicker papers are too rigid for bending and folding. You can get away with using some bond or copy papers (for the neon colors), but they tend to wrinkle and curl, which can be tricky to work with at first.

Large sheets of printmaking paper work really nicely, too. They tend to be more absorbent than stationery papers. You may need to work more quickly and with more saturated colors for bolder prints. You can find these at your local art supply store.

**Tools:** Rubber combs, wood-graining tools, kitchen utensils, skewers, and stamps each create unique marks and patterns. Rubber tools are ideal for paste paper because they are flexible and clean up easily. Be careful with stiffer tools, such as skewers, plastic knives, and metal graining tools; they can tear your paper once it's wet with paint. Look for tools in craft stores and hardware stores in the faux finishing and specialty paint sections.

# THE PROCESS

### STEP 1 MIX THE METHYL CELLULOSE

Methyl cellulose comes in powder form and is mixed with water to create a gel. Read the manufacturer's mixing directions. Usually, you'll dissolve a few tablespoons of powdered methyl cellulose in hot water in a clean jar. Mix thoroughly until all the powder is dissolved, and then add cold water until your container is full. Stir and let the mixture sit to reach a gel consistency.

Ideally, you want to mix your methyl cellulose a few hours in advance. Reserve a jar or two of methyl cellulose ready for printing—one reserved for "clear coats" only and the other to divvy up among your paint pots. If you purchase a large quantity from a bookbinding supply house, mix only the amount you'll use in a single printing session.

### STEP 2 PREPARE THE SURFACE

Prepare your surface by brushing on a layer of methyl cellulose. This first coat is always essential, whether you are working with fresh paper or adding a new layer to already-painted paper. The methyl cellulose primes and lubricates the surface; it also protects the color or pattern of the paper below. If you skip this first clear coat, the paint will absorb into the paper and you won't get a pattern.

### STEP 3 COAT WITH METHYL CELLULOSE

Working fairly quickly, brush on a coat of paint-methyl mixture with a foam brush over the entire surface of your paper. Anywhere you miss will remain unpainted and unpatterned. Don't oversaturate your paper with a thick, goopy coat. Your paper should be wet and shiny, but there should be no standing pools or thick spots.

## MIXING COLORS:

Muffin tins, plastic cups, and wide-mouth jars are good for mixing colors. Add a spoonful or two of methyl cellulose to each of your clean jars, then add paint. A general rule of thumb is about one-third methyl cellulose to two-thirds paint. Mix until combined. Depending on the type of paint, you may need to add more color to your mixture if the paint seems too transparent or thin. Test the color on a scrap of paper. Remember, the color in its wet state will be darker and more vibrant than the color when it's dry. To keep colors such as indigos and brick reds rich, add more paint to the mixture.

Blacks and metallics are the only paints I don't mix with methyl cellulose. I like to use them straight out of the bottle, working quickly for maximum contrast and punch.

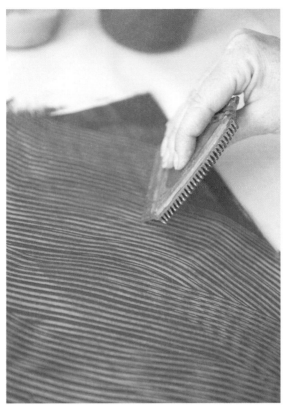

### STEP 4 MAKE THE DESIGN

Using one of your rubber combs, start at the top left and drag the comb from top to bottom over the surface of your paper to create the first bar of your pattern. Move over to the middle of the page and repeat, dragging the comb over the surface of the page. Move to the last portion of the paper and drag your comb again, revealing the paper color below for this two-color paste paper.

You don't have to work from top to bottom every time; you can work diagonally across the page, too. Comb a pattern over the entire page, then go back and re-comb in the opposite direction for a smaller, more detailed pattern. Each tool you use, how much pressure you use, and your own "hand" in using the tool will result in a unique print every time. The rubber combs also create variety in the lines you make: three-sided triangular combs or four-sided square combs usually have a series of teeth in different sizes and spacing. Experiment using a single side, and then combine using multiple sides to make new patterns.

### STEP 5 CLEAN UP

Clean your tools after each print and wipe off the combs with a baby wipe when switching colors. At the end of a printing session, clean all your tools under running water.

# WOOD GRAIN

**Wood-grain tool:** my favorite comb for paste paper.

Using the wood-graining tool is a little trickier than the triangle or square combs because you rock the tool back and forth while dragging it across the surface of the paper. The more you rock the comb, the more circular knots you'll get. Fewer rocks will result in a longer wood grain with a more vertical pattern.

Keep a consistent motion as you pull the comb down to avoid making stopping and starting marks. Give yourself the time and patience to practice. This tool comes with a removable handle. I take out the handle and place my thumb and forefinger into the hole instead. This is more fluid for me, but experiment and see which way works best for you. Creating faux-bois prints is pretty addicting!

## WOOD-GRAIN PLAIDS

An easy way to transform a less-than-amazing print is by adding a second layer. I often do this with a dark layer of paint and the wood-graining tool. The end result is something like a plaid the mad hatter might wear; it's pretty awesome.

Adding a second layer of paint on top of an existing pattern follows the exact same process. Protect your existing print with a layer of clear methyl cellulose, paint a second coat with your paint and methyl-cellulose mixture, and comb in your pattern. You can also create a pattern over already-printed paper such as wallpaper, giftwrap, or scrapbook pages.

*Wood-grain paper*

*Using a triangle comb, create a small pattern of overlapping strokes. Create a pattern in one direction, then comb in the opposite direction for a small, diagonal, check pattern.*

## STEP 1 PREPARE THE SURFACE

Prepare your paper in the same way for all paste paper with a clear coat of methyl cellulose. Paint a second layer with your paint-methyl mixture. Working quickly, begin at the top left of the page and drag and rock the wood-graining comb from the top to the bottom of the page in one continuous long pull. Remember, more rocks equal more knots. Move to the center of the page, and drag and rock the comb from top to bottom. Repeat until the surface of the paper is covered. Practice this motion. You can quickly repaint the surface of this page if you absolutely hate your first try. Just remember that too much re-painting and re-combing can overwork the paper.

Clean your wood-graining tool every time you switch colors or if you have a lot of paint in the grooves of the tool. Sometimes a baby wipe will do the trick, but often I take the tool to the sink and clean it with water and a scrubby brush. Don't be afraid to take a sponge or brush to the tool. If paint dries in the grooves of the tool, it won't make marks. Thoroughly dry off your tool before printing again so you don't introduce water into your print.

# POLKA DOTS

Some rubber combs come with a wavy edge. This is used for making faux malachite, but I use it to make a polka-dotlike print. To make polka dots, press and lift the wavy edge and drag the comb across the paper. Depressing the edge longer as you pull will result in longer, more oval-shaped dots.

*Polka-dot tool*

*Polka dot in process*

*Final polka dot*

# USING BLACKS AND METALLICS

I like blacks and metallics to be as vibrant as possible, so I use them straight out of the bottle (without adding any methyl cellulose). Keep in mind that unmixed colors will absorb faster and you'll need to work quickly.

Once you've primed your paper with a layer of methyl cellulose, squirt a drizzle of paint onto the surface of your page. Use a foam brush to spread the paint until the page is covered. You can always add more paint, but it's harder to remove excess paint. Start with less instead of more. Your coat of paint should be pretty opaque with little to no paper showing through.

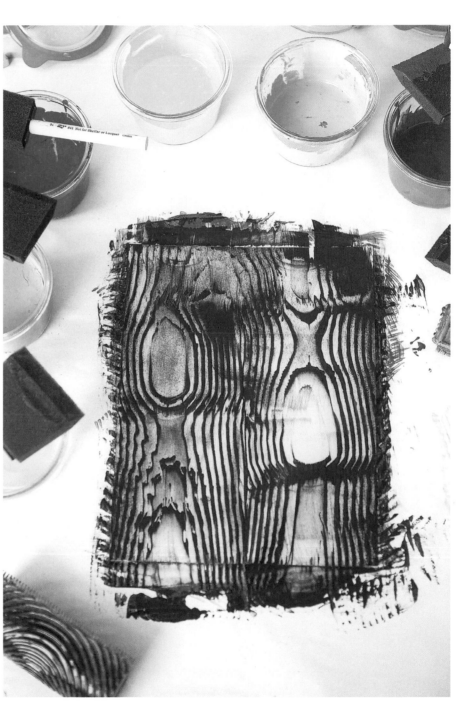

*Using the comb of your choice, create your pattern.*

# PASTE PAPER VARIATIONS

*Wood-grain plaid, pink paint on red paper. Second pass with aqua paint*

*Chocolate on yellow paper. Second pass with bright pink*

*Gold paint on aqua paper*

*Gold paint on black paper*

*Aqua paint on antique-gold paper*

*Aqua paint on neon coral paper*

*Wood-grain plaid, red (with a smidge of gold) paint on aqua paper. Second pass with a deep eggplant paint*

*Wood-grain plaid, black paint on copper paper. Second pass with gold paint*

*Wood-grain plaid, dark red paint on aqua paper. Second pass with gold paint*

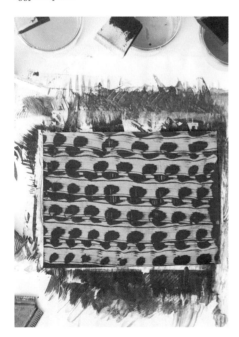

*Black paint on curry yellow paper*

*Wood-grain plaid, raspberry paint on chartreuse paper. Second pass with a royal-blue, Golden Fluid acrylic paint*

*Create a sample sheet of paint colors and how they mix optically when overlapped. Test color combinations before working on final projects.*

# CREDIT CARD PAINTING

Using a credit card to apply paint is quick and satisfying. While this method is free form, the credit card's rigidity and hard edges give uniformity and structure to the mark making.

To paint using a credit card, simply dip or scoop paint with the edge of the card. Apply slight pressure while dragging the card in a straight line, much like a squeegee. This will result in a thin, flat, even band of color. Apply more paint as needed. Switch colors easily by wiping the card with a baby wipe or paper towel.

# MARK MAKING

When I created window displays at Anthropologie, I learned how to take a single small object or motif and make an impact by using hundreds (or thousands) of them instead of just a few. Massing things with multiples and repetition can create an intentional and eye-catching presentation. Think of a handful of clothespins versus an undulating mass of hundreds. The same principle applies to two-dimensional forms and even to simple marks made with a pencil, marker, or brush. A single line is just a line, but a single line drawn a hundred or a thousand times makes a repeating pattern.

Simple shapes or strokes create impact when repeated, and hand-drawn lines have a beautiful irregularity. Using a brush or a brush tip marker allows you to apply pressure when making each stoke to create even more variety within each line. Dots and dashes are a classic go-to mark. Play with scale, size, and precision for different effects. These are some of my favorite shapes to draw when creating patterns on paper and fabric.

*Here are some of my favorite marks and shapes for making patterns.*

*When using ink and paint, overlap colors to create new color combinations. I especially love the way neon colors interact with more muted tones for unexpected combinations.*

# PROJECTS TO PLAY WITH:
## creating patterns and surfaces for everyday designs

# COLOR STUDY PAINTING

This approach to painting is loose, fast, and playful. Experiment with quick marks, swatches of color, and unexpected combinations. Create a large canvas to hang over a sofa, or use a faux headboard above a bed. This technique can be modified to any scale and used on any surface that accepts paint.

## MATERIALS

Wooden panel or canvas

Credit card

Variety of acrylic paints

Baby wipes (optional)

### STEP 1

Make a mark. Begin by adding paint to the panel. Paint patches in this first color in three to five spots on the canvas. Vary their shape and size.

### STEP 2

Continue adding patches of color, allowing each color to dry before moving to the next layer to avoid mixing and muddying the colors.

*Note: Use baby wipes to clean the credit card (and your hands) between color changes.*

### STEP 3

The same method was used for both of these paintings. The peach, blue, and teal was created by painting the surface of the panel once. The painting on the easel was painted with several layers, some of which were wet while new layers were added and scraped to create striations.

# PASTE PAPER MOBILE

Circles of sea-colored paper sway gently from a piece of driftwood collected during a sunset walk along the beach. Bring the feeling of the salty sea home without the gritty sand.

## MATERIALS

Sheets of paste paper

2-inch (5 cm) circle punch

Metallic sewing thread

Sewing needle

Driftwood or found branch

### STEP 1

Using paper punches is a quick and easy way to cut circles from your sheets of paste paper. Flipping the punch allows you to frame a section of paper before punching. Punch twenty-five to thirty circles from a variety of paste papers.

### STEP 2

Using a sewing needle and about 3 feet (1 m) of metallic thread, string each circle of paper onto the length of your thread. Place the first paper circle at the bottom of the thread and secure into place by re-entering the top hole and looping around the edge of the circle. Continue stringing paper circles until you have six or seven circles spaced 1 inch (2.5 cm) or so apart.

### STEP 3

With an extra foot (30 cm) or so of thread, wrap the cord around the branch and secure into place.

### STEP 4

Continue stringing 3-foot (1 m) lengths of thread until you have five on the branch. Hang the branch with an additional thread or a small nail.

# STUDY IN CIRCLES: TEA TOWELS

Soft circles and dots in primary colors add the perfect pattern to any cotton tea towel. A set of these make a great gift and pair perfectly with a favorite recipe or cookbook.

## MATERIALS

Yellow Owl Workshop ink pads or fabric-safe ink pads

Bubble wrap

Cotton tea towels

Iron

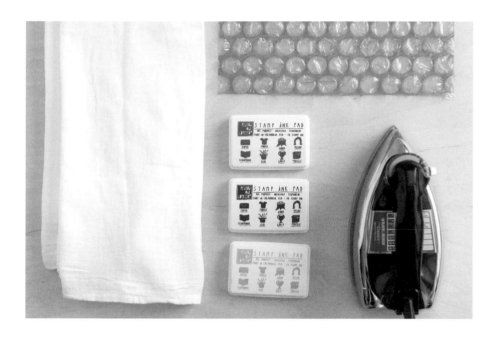

### STEP 1

Using bubble wrap allows you to create a pattern of circles with soft edges. The cotton tea towels further add to the soft and subtle beauty of this print. Try playing with color combinations or overlapping prints for a variation. Change the pattern within the bubble wrap by selectively popping bubbles.

### STEP 2

Tap the ink pad over the surface of the bubble wrap until well inked. This may require two passes.

### STEP 3

Carefully place the bubble wrap facedown onto the blank tea towel and press. I like to print right to the edge, so you may want to work on newsprint or other protected surface.

**STEP 4**

Repeat steps 2 and 3 to create a continuous print. Play with alignment, leaving blank space or popping bubbles for various effects.

**STEP 5**

For permanence and washability, heat-set the ink per the manufacturer's instructions. When done printing, rinse the bubble wrap of any ink residue and save for future projects.

*Note: When changing ink colors, be sure to rinse and thoroughly dry the bubble wrap before re-inking.*

Using ink pads and bubble wrap creates quick, lovely monoprints. Printing on paper will yield bolder, brighter prints while printing on fabric results in softer prints. Using bubble wrap creates structure by limiting the motif to circles or dots to create your patterns, allowing you to focus on color choice, material, and placement. Bubble wrap monoprints have clean, finished designs, but they are also great for creating backgrounds for other printing and collage work.

# PAINTED PILLOW COVER

There is something so liberating about painting on a huge canvas or piece of fabric, and then cutting it into smaller pieces, creating new unexpected compositions. This half-and-half pillow cover is the perfect balance of wild color and its neutral counterpart. Play with making marks with paint, and then add structure by pairing it with a solid fabric for a pillow that will work in any room.

## MATERIALS

*(Makes an 18-inch [45 cm] square pillow)*

18-inch (45 cm) square pillow form

19 x 10-inch (47.5 x 26 cm) piece of painted cotton fabric, using the credit card method (see page 32)

19 x 10-inch (47.5 x 26 cm) piece of linen or other solid fabric

Two 19 x 19-inch (47.5 x 47.5 cm) pieces of fabric for the back (I used denim, but any woven fabric will do.)

Sewing machine and thread

Pins

Iron

Create the front panel of the pillow by aligning the linen and painted fabric with right sides facing. Sew with a ¼-inch (6 mm) seam allowance, backstitching at the beginning and end. Press the seam to one side to prepare for assembling the pillow later.

**STEP 2**

Prepare the back panels by sewing a ½-inch (12 mm) hem on each. Fold over the long edge of the fabric and press with an iron. Fold over again and pin in place. Sew the hem, stitching along the inner edge of the hem. Repeat on the second back panel.

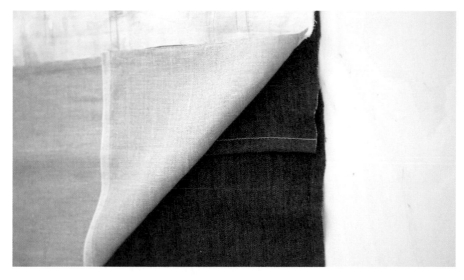

### STEP 3

Arrange the layers of the pillow so that the two back panels overlap, both with right sides facing up. This is an envelope closure like the one used for the Stamped-Envelope Keepsake Pouches (see page 111). Depending on the loft of the pillow, you may want a deeper or shallower overlap and will need to adjust your fabric accordingly.

### STEP 4

Place the front panel facedown, and align and pin. The right sides should be facing inward for all the panels.

### STEP 5

Sew the layers together using a generous seam allowance, around 1 inch (2.5 cm). Depending on how squishy the pillow stuffing is, you might want a tighter or looser fit. The style of closure is great because you can re-sew and trim away any excess seam allowance until you get the perfect fit.

# FRAMED PHOTO MATS

Framing a special photograph with patterned paper adds dimension and interest. Pair a bold print with a graphic photo. Or choose a soft and subtle pattern for a sweet, vintage image.

## MATERIALS

Paste paper in a variety of sizes, any weight (see page 21)

Photo frames

Photos

Washi tape, double-sided tape, or photo-mounting corners

### STEP 1

Tear or cut the paste paper to fit the frame. Mount the photo onto the paste paper using double-sided tape for an invisible mount. Add washi tape or photo corners for a decorative presentation. Cluster several frames for an instant collection.

*Tone-on-tone patterns make a beautiful, subtle backdrop to any photo.*

# COLOR PLAY LAMPSHADE

This is a free-form painting technique, but using a credit card as your brush creates uniform marks that give structure to the chaos. The result is a painterly look that is modern and fresh.

## MATERIALS

Light-colored lampshade with smooth sides (Avoid anything with tucks, pleats, or heavy texture.)

Credit card or library card

Acrylic craft paints in a variety of colors

## STEP 1

Starting with your lightest color anywhere on the shade, squeeze a dime-size amount of paint onto the shade. Using the credit card, press and scrape paint in a vertical stroke. Add paint and squeegee paint until you form a mark you like.

## STEP 2

Working in the same color, continue making painted marks on the shade. Create several patches in the first color and allow to dry.

## STEP 3

Select a new color and repeat steps 1 and 2. Vary the sizes of the patches you make on this round. Allow the paint to dry.

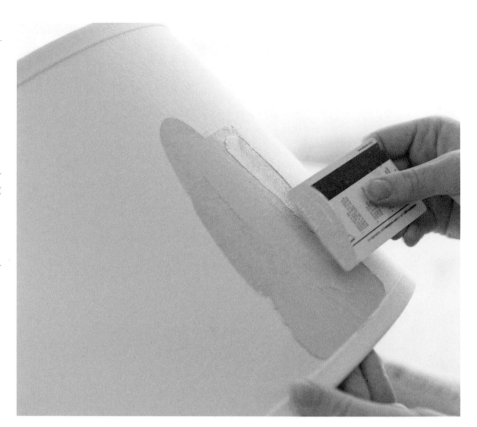

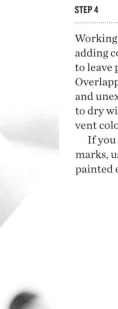

## STEP 4

Working from lightest to darkest, continue adding color patches on the shade. Feel free to leave patches of the shade fabric showing. Overlapping colors will result in interesting and unexpected colors. Allowing each color to dry will give you cleaner results and prevent colors from becoming muddy.

If you like cleaner-edged patches and marks, use your credit card to clean up painted edges.

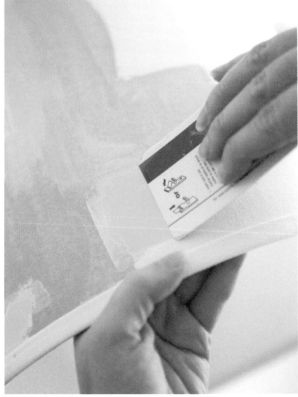

# PAINTED LEATHER COASTERS

These leather coasters are fun and quick to make. They are the perfect cocktail party accessory and make a great hostess gift. Change up the color palette for a variation on this look. Indigo and golds would be dazzling on the nude leather, while black, white, and neons would be bright and bold.

## MATERIALS

4-inch (10 cm) leather circle blanks

Leather paint

Paintbrush

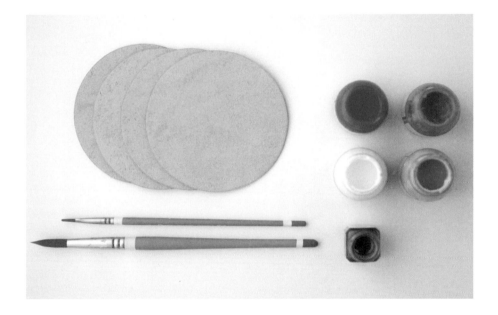

## STEP 1

On the smooth side of the leather, paint your first layer of color. Leather paints often come with their own brush inside the bottle. The paint is thick and viscous, allowing you to get opaque, even coverage with just one coat. Starting with your lightest color (white), apply a patch of color to the leather.

I like irregular edges and a loose painting style for this process. Because the edges are soft and organic, I like to keep my strokes consistent, painting in only one direction.

## STEP 2

Apply your next color in the same way as you did for your first layer. If your brush isn't small enough for detail painting, switch to a small-tip brush instead.

**STEP 3**

Continue adding colors of paint, varying the sizes of patches you paint onto the coaster. Look to balance the size and the colors so that your eye moves around the coaster. Avoid making all the patches the same size and shape. Play with size and scale for a dynamic pattern.

**STEP 4**

For an added bit of glam, add a metallic paint or even a patch of gold leaf to the coaster. When adding metallic, I'll often use an enamel paint designed for model trains to create a dense metallic finish. The enamel and leather paints work well together and, best of all, don't need any sealing before using the coaster!

# BOLD BOTANICAL PRINTS

These bright, botanical prints are a modern take on a classic cyanotype-like print. Pair swathes of neon paint with delicate textures and shapes in deep indigo for an updated look.

## MATERIALS

Gelatin printing surface (see page 11)

Brayer

Speedball printing ink in denim blue

Variety of papers with patches of color, using the credit card method (see page 32)

Leaves and plants

### STEP 1

Roll a layer of ink onto the surface of the gelatin.

### STEP 2

Place a leaf onto the surface of the gelatin and carefully lay paper over the top. Gently press around the leaf. Pull off the page to reveal your first print. These modern botanical prints are meant to be bold with high contrast, so we won't pull a second print from this impression. Remove the leaf and re-ink the surface of the gelatin for each print.

*Note: If you don't have denim or indigo blue ink, you can mix primary blue with a hint of yellow and a smidge of black for a denim look. Replace the yellow with black for a warmer, more indigo, hue.*

Western Meadowlark

Mountain Bluebird

*forever*
USA

*forever*
USA

*forever*
USA

*forever*
USA

Evening Grosbeak

Scarlet Tanager

# SAND AND SEA NOTECARDS

Using just two bands of colors, these simple painted marks evoke a landscape almost immediately. Paint something in just a few minutes without even breaking out the palette and brushes.

## MATERIALS

Set of flat notecards and coordinating envelopes (I'm using White and Pool from Paper Source in an A7 size)

Acrylic paint in two sea colors (indigo blue and aqua green) and one sand color (blush)

Credit card

## STEP 1

Dip the credit card into the sand-color paint on one side of the edge of the credit card. Dip the other side into the sea-color paint. Make sure the paint covers the entire edge of the card. Otherwise, you'll have a white strip down the middle of the pattern.

## STEP 2

With the credit card loaded with paint, gently press and drag the credit card down one-quarter to one-third of the edge of the notecard. If you didn't load up the credit card with enough paint, don't worry. Just reload and go over your painted edge. Play with how saturated the color is and how the pattern is created by varying the amount of paint and the amount of pressure you impose when you drag the card down the side of the notecard.

*Try randomly loading your credit card with paint for an unexpected pattern.*

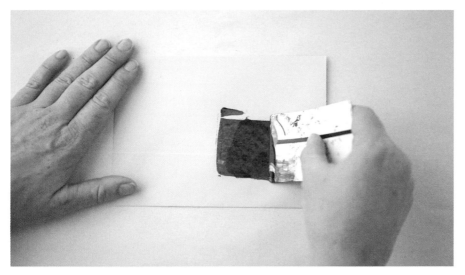

Repeat steps 1 and 2 for each card. You can use two or three colors at once, or switch up how you pair your paints. The notecards will be ready to use in minutes because acrylic dries quickly and you are applying a thin coat of paint.

*For an extra punch of color, use your credit card to apply a quick swatch of paint to your envelopes.*

*If using dark paint, address envelopes with a metallic or neon pen.*

# MODERN BLACK-AND-WHITE BOOK COVERS

Covering books reminds me of being a kid and getting ready to go back to school in the fall. These painted book covers are the contemporary counterparts to the grocery bag covers you might recall from childhood. Channel your inner child to paint large-scale graphics, then discard any further thoughts of kindergarten. The monochromatic palette and repetition of marks create a sophisticated and dramatic finished cover perfect for a stack of books or even every book on your shelf!

## MATERIALS

Large sketch paper (60 lb, or 89 gsm)

Sumi ink or other acrylic ink

Fine-point watercolor brush (small to medium point)

Coarse-bristled brush

Small containers for ink and water

## STEP 1

Lightly dip the tip of the coarse-bristled brush into a bowl of ink. With very gentle pressure, drag the brush across the surface of the paper. The key is to let the brush do the work. Every time you dip the brush into the ink, the bristles will separate in a random pattern that will then create a unique mark on the page. Create stripes, cross hatch, random vertical marks, or pivot the brush in place to create circles. Re-ink the brush as needed. Create a drybrush stripe by lightly dipping the tip of a coarse-bristled brush into a bowl of ink and gently dragging over the surface.

## STEP 2

To create smaller, delicate patterns, use a fine-point watercolor brush. Experiment with line quality by changing the pressure on the brush. Pressing down will create fatter, thicker lines. Painting with the tip at a 90-degree angle from the page with light pressure will create fine lines. Paint lines that fluctuate from thick to thin, and make Vs or Xs or tiny circles for small-scale prints.

*Note: For a variety of black and gray shades, mix a little water in the bowl with the ink. Sumi ink goes on dark and can dry much lighter, so experiment with saturation.*

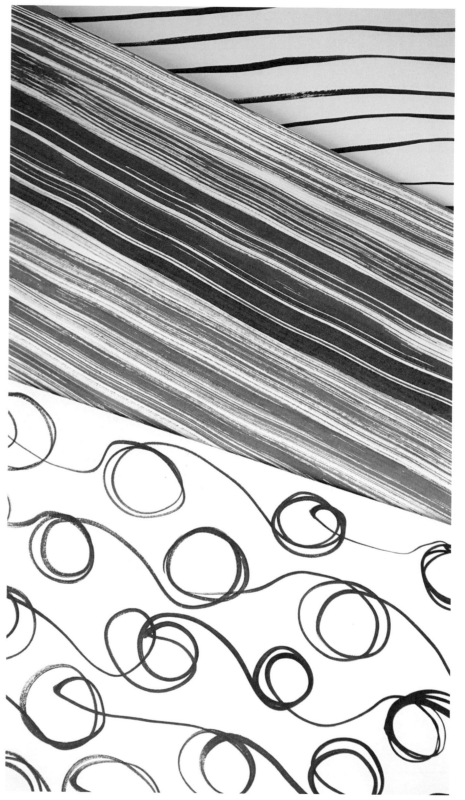

*Stripes, drybrush, and loops*

*Circles, Vs, and drybrush*

*Xs, pebbles, and circles*

# PATTERNED NOTEBOOKS

These little notebooks are perfect to take along on your day-to-day travels. Tuck one into your bag for yourself or give one as a gift. They are easy to use and fun to make.

## MATERIALS

8½ x 5½-inch (21.3 x 13.8 cm) sheets of paste paper in a cover or cardstock weight, 1 per book (see page 21)

8¼ x 5¼-inch (20.6 x 13 cm) sheets of lined or blank text-weight paper, 10 per book

Waxed linen thread

Bookbinding or sewing needle

### STEP 1

Fold the inner papers in half to create a signature. Fold the cover in half.

### STEP 2

To bind the book, cut a piece of waxed linen thread three times the length of the spine.

### STEP 3

Begin in the inside of the book. Pierce a hole in the center of the spine-fold, and pull the needle and thread through, leaving a 3- to 4-inch (7.5 to 10 cm) tail.

Coming from the outside of the book, pierce a hole in the outer spine about an inch (2.5 cm) from the edge and pull the thread taut through to the inside cover.

Skip the center hole and make the last hole in the center fold on the other side of the center, about 1 inch (2.5 cm) from the edge. Pull the thread to the outside, then come back through the center hole once more to end where you started. You make a sort of pretzel shape with the sewn binding.

**STEP 5**

With the tail you left and the remaining thread, tie a double knot over the center stitch to secure in place.

*Note: Where you start sewing is where your final knot or bow will be. You can start on the outside of the book if you want to have a decorative bow on the outside.*

# MAKING MARKS POSTCARDS

These index-card postcards are inexpensive, fun to make, and quick to draw. Experiment with shapes, color, and line quality. Once you start making these, you won't be able to walk out the door without a stack of blank cards and a bag full of markers!

## MATERIALS

Index cards or 4 x 6-inch (10 x 15 cm) cardstock cards

Markers, pens, and colored pencils

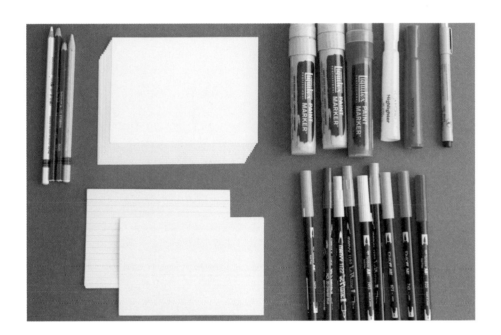

**STEP 1**

Create a background using a broad-tipped paint marker. Work in a medium to light color so you can layer over this first pass. Be sure to color or draw off the edge of the postcard; avoid the urge to just fill in the center of the card.

**STEP 2**

Start layering in smaller details. Use line work to create visual interest and intimacy. Play with using various mediums such as markers and colored pencils. Begin to develop your color palette.

### STEP 3

Working in smaller patches and in a brighter color, add a second layer of color fields. Using a neon over a dull neutral allows the neon to really pop. The pairing of a bright color with a subdued color creates interest.

### STEP 4

Create your last round of marks. I used a red, which is a primary color; it relates with the thin blue lines, while both conflict a little with the color fields in the background. I love the activation it creates visually, pairing colors you wouldn't necessarily put together initially.

   Create a suite of postcards in a variety of color palettes. Play with different mark-making techniques and combinations. Consider the size and scale of your marks, repetition, and asymmetrical patterns.

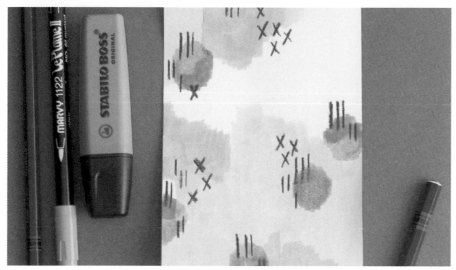

# SCRIBBLE GARLAND

Making seemingly random marks over and over can create a beautiful, haphazard design. Peel-away labels act as tiny individual canvases within the scribbled page that, when strung together, create a fresh and festive garland. Pair these free-form patterns with bold solids for a dynamic design.

**MATERIALS**

Office paper labels in white or cream

Markers, paint pens, and colored pencils

Solid color office labels

Twine, ribbon, or string

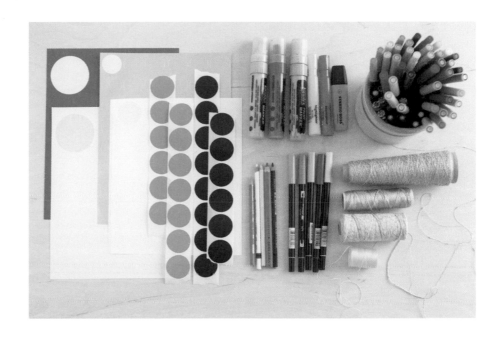

### STEP 1

Create a loose first layer, coloring randomly over the sheet of labels. It's always easier to work from the lightest color to the darkest, but this is a really forgiving process, so don't overthink your marks.

### STEP 2

Add a second layer, placing smaller patches of color randomly on the page.

### STEP 3

Liven up your scribble by adding bold colors in various mediums. I used a neon pink highlighter and a deep, creamy, indigo pencil to create smaller, scratchier marks that add texture and detail.

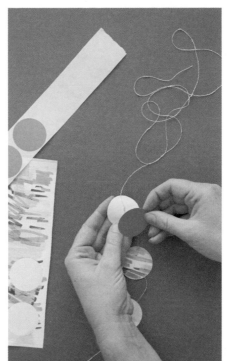

## STEP 4

Using a length of string or twine, begin placing your labels to create a festive garland. Place a single scribble label over a solid label, sandwiching the thread in the middle of the circle. You can mix up your labels by layering solids on solids or scribbles on scribbles. Avoid making a perfect pattern. Carefully align your labels for the best results!

Add these festive garlands to any corner of your home for a pop of color and pattern. Consider draping them over frames, in a doorway, or down a table for instant décor.

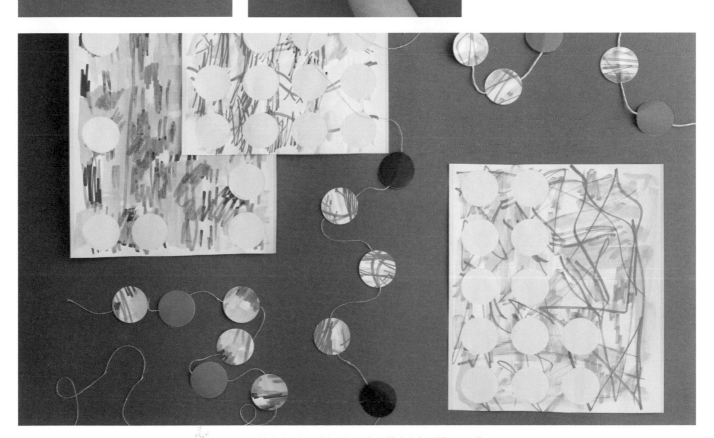

*Make a set of garlands using a variety of color palettes and labels. Play with using colored labels for different effects.*

# MARBLED BANGLES

Chunky bangles are marbled with soft veins of color or bold neons to pack a punch. Pair a statement bangle with a neutral garment for a modern twist on a traditional look.

## MATERIALS

A variety of nail polish in your color choice (I'm using an aqua, blue, and peach.)

Blank wooden bangles

Bowl of water at least 4-inches (10 cm) deep

Paper towels

Bamboo or wooden skewers

Waxed paper or cookie sheet (optional)

### STEP 1

Place a few drops of nail polish in your first color in a bowl of water. Most of the polish will float to the surface. The color will look pale at this point.

Add a few drops of polish in your next two colors, one at a time. It doesn't matter if you drop polish in the center or on the side; you're going to mix it all up in a minute.

### STEP 2

Working quickly, use a wooden skewer to gently swirl a pattern into the polish. Drag the skewer from side to side across the bowl, or in the middle to create a pattern. Play with how the color mixes. You don't want to overmix because the polish will start to form a skin that is hard to print with.

### STEP 3

With your swirled pattern in place, gently dip and roll the bangle into the bowl. You'll see the swirled pattern adhere to the bangle immediately. If you wait too long, the remaining skin on the surface of the water will start to lift off the water. You can add on more layers if needed, switching to a darker polish and reprinting. Repeat steps 1 and 2, allowing bangle to dry on a paper towel about for about fifteen minutes, or until polish is no longer tacky. Clean up remaining polish with paper towel. Remove any polish on the bowl with acetone, and then wash with soap and water.

I recommend only pulling one print at a time to avoid getting muddy patterns and color. Add new polish and swirl a new pattern rather than trying to use up little bits of remaining polish after you've printed. Clean the surface of your water by dragging a paper towel over the remaining polish.

Once you've printed your bangle, the surface of the bracelet will be tacky because we're using an oil and water process. Allow your bangle to dry on waxed paper or other nonporous surface for about an hour. If you have any globs or thick spots, you can gently pat them down with a damp paper towel. If you had a lot of air bubbles in the process of printing, you may get a little flaking of polish when you wear the bracelet. You can easily seal your marbled pattern with a spray varnish before wearing.

You'll find that the immediate and vibrant result of this process is addicting, and you'll soon be gathering items around your house to marble.

Feel free to experiment with color and pattern, adding more colors of polish and using various swirling techniques. Try marbling glass and ceramic, wood and metal, or even paper. Using nail polish is fun because it is accessible and the colors are fantastic, but in the long term it can be an expensive option. Consider using a marbling kit when marbling many objects or large surfaces.

# STAMPED GIFTWRAP

Truth be told, I love wrapping presents, and I use every one of the methods in this book on paper for giftwrap. Stamped giftwrap is one of my favorite ways to make unusual, custom paper.

## MATERIALS

Woodblock stamps

Water-based printing ink

Palette or plate for ink

Upholstery foam scrap

18 x 24-inch (45 x 60 cm) sheets of text-weight paper in a variety of colors

*Note: You can substitute rubber stamps and stamping ink, or carve your own stamps from linoleum or Easy Carve in lieu of the woodblocks. I used to use rubber stamps all the time, but the print quality of the woodblocks is much closer to the look of traditional printmaking and it has a textural quality that rubber stamping doesn't. Woodblocks are easier to use when working with ink and especially good for getting bold, saturated color when printing on fabric.*

### STEP 1

Set up a palette of color by scooping print-ing ink onto a plate or other flat surface. Ink in a jar tends to be looser than ink in a tube (either will work). Spread ink onto the palette surface so that it lies flat.

### STEP 2

Ink the woodblock by dabbing the foam cube into the ink. Tap lightly several times until the surface of the foam is fully inked. Using the same tapping motion, apply a thin and even coat of ink to the surface of the woodblock stamp.

Stamp a motif. Firmly press the stamp, ink-side down, onto the paper. Don't rock or shift the stamp. Using woodblock stamps prevents most printing mishaps common with rubber stamping, such as smearing and double lines. Re-ink the stamp after every impression.

**STEP 4**

Create a pattern. Consider placing stamped motifs randomly and with no orientation in lines or columns, or in an asymmetrical design.

*Note: Work within an established color palette for a suite of coordinating wrap.*

# MARBLED BAMBOO PARTY PLATES

These dreamy plates are both delicate and bold. Little veins of concentrated color meander across a neutral wooden plate for pieces that will create movement across any tablescape.

## MATERIALS

Bamboo party plates or wooden plates in various sizes

Large bowl of water

Several bottles of nail polish

Bamboo skewers

Acetone and paper towels for cleanup

### STEP 1

Drop several drops of nail polish onto the surface of the water, using two or three colors.

### STEP 2

Swirl the polish to create a pattern. Remember, this can be loose and free.

### STEP 3

Working quickly, dip one side of a bamboo plate into the bowl of water. You can dip straight up and down, or come in from the side of the bowl at an angle if you want to float the pattern onto the middle of the plate.

If you still have polish, rotate the plate and re-dip plate.

**STEP 5**

Clean the surface of the water between dipping each plate by running a paper towel along the water. Repeat steps 1 through 4 for each plate you wish to print. Allow the plates to dry thoroughly before using. These plates are only good for dry foods unless sealed with a spray acrylic varnish.

I prefer to "cure" and seal the plates with a bit of olive oil. Simply rub a little oil onto each plate with a paper towel and gently buff away.

*Note: Metallic polishes and very thin layers of polish can flake off. Use a paper towel to gently buff away any flaking paint, then seal with acrylic spray varnish.*

# WATERCOLOR RIBBONS

Transform a solid satin ribbon into a riot of color for a look that feels hand-dyed but takes a fraction of the time.

## MATERIALS

A variety of double-faced satin ribbons

Fabric and textile paint in chosen colors

Paintbrushes in varying widths

Iron (optional)

## STEP I

Roll out a section of ribbon at a time and begin painting. Experiment with drybrush painting, dabbing a little bit of paint on the tip of a wide brush and gently dragging the brush over the ribbon in short strokes (shown bottom package, left). Combine contrasting indigo and hot pink paints for a striking design (shown middle package, left). Paint dots of pink color against larger strokes of indigo. Play with mark making to create various watercolor affects (shown top and middle package, left). Apply paint thinly avoiding thick globs. Allow each layer of color to dry to avoid muddy mixing. Allow paint to dry completely before using the ribbons. If using ribbons for something other than wrapping, heat-set the fabric paint according to the manufacturer's specifications.

# CELEBRATION GARLAND

Any time is a good time to celebrate . . .

## MATERIALS

A variety of paste paper sheets on text-weight paper (see page 21)

3-inch (7.5 cm) scalloped craft punch or other shaped punch

Long needle

Embroidery thread or yarn

Paper straws

Scissors

Paint- and coarse-bristled brush (optional)

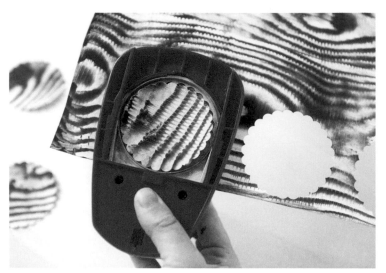

*Use a variety of shades within a particular color palette for a subtle shift in color.*

### STEP I

Punch scalloped circles out of your paste paper. You can use a mix of colors or select a range of a single color. For a 4-foot (1.2 m) strand, I used about one hundred scalloped circles.

### STEP 2

Optional: If you want to create your own design or colored paper straws, use the dry brush technique (see step 1, page 70) to quickly transform your paper straws. Allow the straws to dry completely before cutting them into beads.

### STEP 3

Cut the paper straws into ¼- to ½-inch (6 to 12 mm) sections to create paper beads. The longer your paper beads, the more space between each of your scalloped circles. For a 4-foot (1.3 m) garland, I used about five paper straws, but these paper beads are so easy to make and use, you might as well make a few extra.

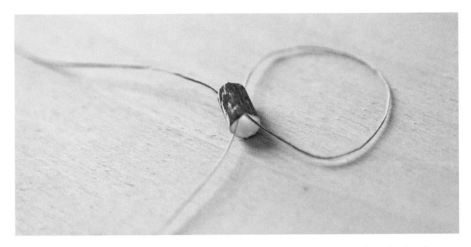

String the garland starting with a paper bead, then piercing a scalloped circle in the middle and stringing it on. Continue alternating with a bead and then a paper circle until you've reached a length of garland you like. Once all the circles and beads are in place, slide them to the center and tie off each end of the garland by looping your thread around the outside of the last bead, back through the center, then tying off.

*To secure the beginning and end of the garland, string the bead onto the thread, then loop the thread through the bead a second time, catching it in place.*

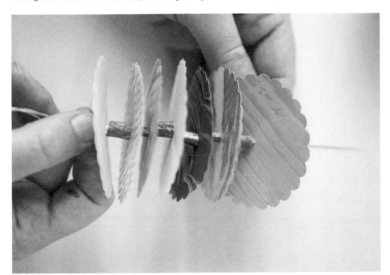

*Mix colors and patterns for a playful or a more sophisticated look.*

# MARBLED TASSELS

Marbling chunky wooden beads is quick and satisfying. Experiment with plain wooden beads or primary-colored ones from the toy store. Use beads to make necklaces, ornaments, or these fabulous tassels!

## MATERIALS

A selection of marbled wooden beads (using the marbling technique shown on page 86)

Yarn, ribbon, or thick twine

Scissors

## STEP 1

Cut several dozen strips of yarn to twice the length of whatever you want your final tassel length to be. Usually thirty strips of yarn about 8-inches (20 cm) long is a good place to start. Take one piece of yarn and place it in the middle of the bundle to tie the bundle in half, leaving a long tail.

## STEP 2

Feed the two ends of the tail through the bead and pull until you have a nice ball of yarn above the bead and the tassel tails below the bead. The tassel will pop through the bead. Pull hard enough to get the tassel through snugly. If you break the yarn, you may have too many lengths in the bundle. Experiment with what works for the opening in your bead and the amount of yarn in your tassel.

# WATERCOLOR SCARF

Creating your own garments and accessories is thrilling! I'm not a particularly adept sewer, but I love that I can whip up a quick scarf that is painterly and bright in no time at all. This technique is forgiving and looks fabulous no matter what approach you take, and the sewing is minimal!

## MATERIALS

1 yard (90 cm) cotton voile fabric

Paintbrush

Fabric paints in a variety of colors

Sewing machine and thread

Iron

Scissors

**STEP 1**

Before you paint the fabric, prepare the yardage by sewing a hem. Determine the length of your scarf. For a single loop I used roughly 1 yard (90 cm) of fabric (double that if you want a double-wrap scarf). Fold over the raw edge of you scarf about ¼ inch (6 mm), and press into place with a hot iron. Fold the edge over again and press a second time to trap in the raw edge.

**STEP 2**

Using a straight stitch, stitch along the center of your pressed hem to finish. Repeat for the other side of the scarf. Do not sew the scarf into a loop yet; you'll want to paint it first.

**STEP 3**

Lay the fabric out on a protected surface and beginning painting. Using a paintbrush, apply patches of color, starting with one color and randomly placing patches over the entire surface. Allow this first layer to dry.

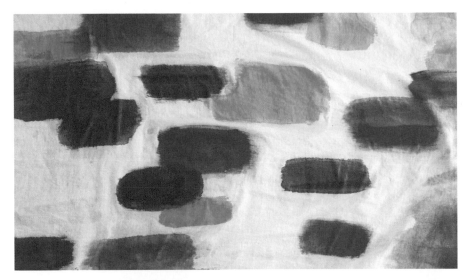

Using a new color, paint a second layer of randomly placed patches over the entire surface. Consider making these patches larger or smaller than the first layer. See what happens when the patches overlap slightly. You might get some really interesting optical color mixing. Allow the second layer to dry. Avoid painting over wet paint. This mixing will cause muddy colors instead of unexpected tertiary colors.

**STEP 5**

Repeat step 4 until you have several layers of colorful patches covering the surface of the fabric. You don't need to fill in the entire surface of the scarf with patches. In fact, leaving a significant amount of unpainted white fabric will make the color patches pop.

**STEP 6**

Once the fabric is completely painted and dry, heat-set the fabric using an iron according to the paint manufacturer's directions.

**STEP 7**

With right sides together, align the fabric and sew the short ends of the fabric together using a ½-inch (12 mm) seam to create the infinity scarf. Wash the scarf separately by hand or on delicate in the washing machine to remove any paint residue. This will soften the painted scarf for wearing.

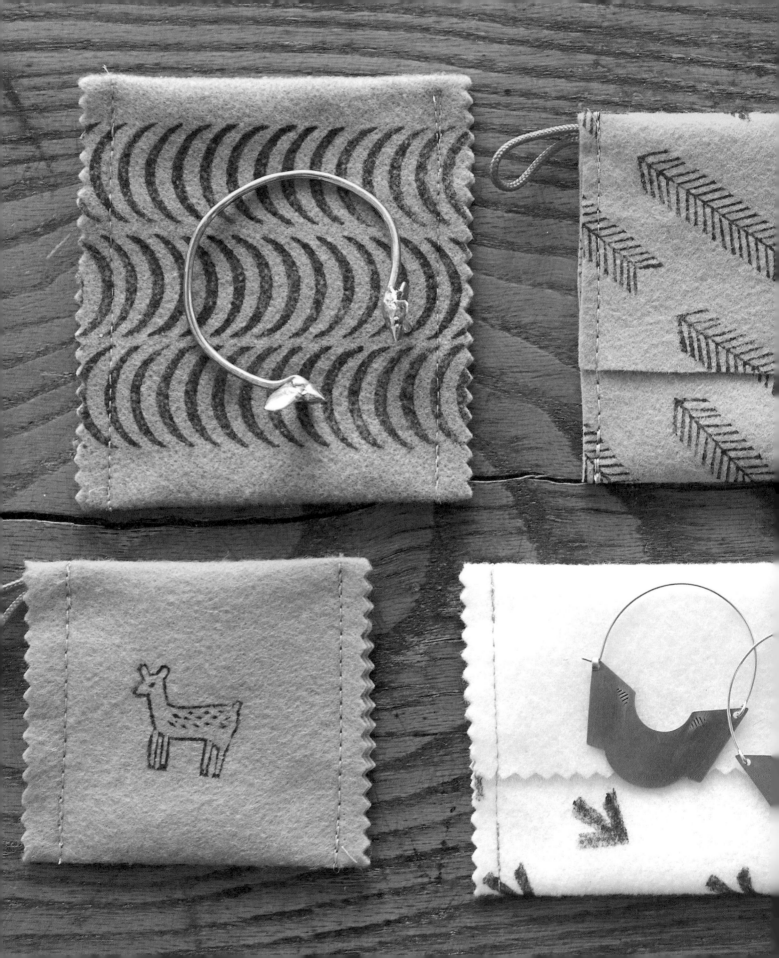

# STAMPED-ENVELOPE KEEPSAKE POUCHES

I used to use rubber stamps to create cards, stationery, and even giftwrap. In the last few years I discovered hand-carved wooden stamps. Although both use similar techniques, the results when using wood stamps are much more like traditional printmaking methods. Using viscous printing inks instead of stamp pads creates juicy opaque colors and images that are vibrant, bold, and oh-so-satisfying. These keepsake pouches are the perfect handmade addition to any gift of jewelry or to protect any tiny treasure. Use them as packaging, for storage or when traveling.

## MATERIALS

Wool felt in a variety of medium to light colors

Woodblock stamps

Scrap of upholstery foam

Fabric paint or screen-printing ink

Ceramic or glass plate

Sewing machine

Neon thread

Pinking shears

Neon cord or thread (optional)

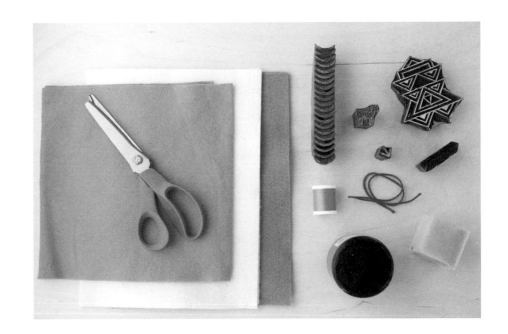

### STEP 1

Scoop or squeeze a dollop of paint onto a plate. Using a small cube of upholstery foam, tap the foam into the paint to evenly disperse. The upholstery foam may seem like an odd material, but the tiny pores of the foam work better than a kitchen sponge or other applicator for dispersing the paint evenly. You can rinse and reuse the foam indefinitely. Foam is available at most fabric stores and upholstery shops. You can often pick up scraps for free and you only need a small chunk.

### STEP 2

Once you've loaded the foam with a bit of paint, lightly tap paint over the entire surface of the wooden stamp. You want a thin, even coat.

### STEP 3

Practice stamping on a scrap of felt until you have the right amount of paint.

To stamp, place the stamp facedown and press firmly. The great thing about wooden stamps is they are solid; you can't rock them back and forth as you can a rubber stamp, which is a common mistake and results in blurry images. The felt also provides just enough cushion when stamping for a clean impression.

### STEP 4

Once you're happy with your technique, begin stamping the felt. You'll need to re-ink the stamp every time you stamp. Create an allover pattern by stamping the motif over the entire surface of the fabric, or center a large motif for a focal image.

These pouches are quick to whip up, so I usually print several sheets of felt using a variety of stamps. Allow yourself to play with the placement of motifs and combine stamps for a variety of patterns. Once you've printed all the felt you need, allow the fabric to dry. If you want to switch to a different color of ink, rinse the stamp and blot dry before switching to a new ink color.

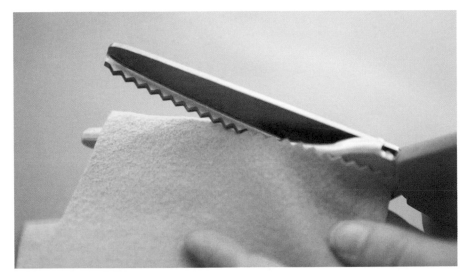

*Stamp an allover pattern to coordinate with a pouch using a single motif. Mix and match for a complete set.*

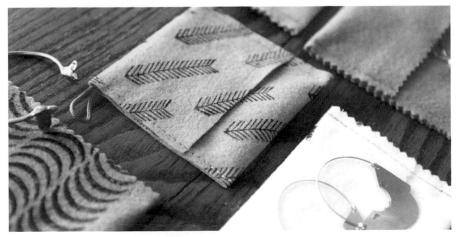

*It's all about the presentation. These stamped pouches work for any small treasure. In addition to being a beautiful wrapping, they are great for storing and traveling with your keepsakes.*

## STEP 5

You can make your pouch in almost any size or shape. Consider what you'll be placing inside. Do you want a rectangle pouch for a pair of glasses, a small square pouch for bracelet, or a tiny pouch for a locket or ring? You can center a large motif on the front of the pouch, or allow the motifs to fall as they will when you stitch everything together.

The beauty of the envelope closure is the overlapping opening. The bottom half of the opening should come up about halfway, while the top should overlap about two-thirds of the way down. Arrange your pouch so the opening is overlapping and you're happy with the way the print falls. If you want to pink the edge of the opening, do that now, before you sew the pouch sides.

## STEP 6

A straight seam on either side of the pouch holds everything in place, and the felt requires no hemming. You can place a pin to hold things in place, but these are a really manageable size to sew without pins. The side seams will get pinked after the pouch is finished.

Using a straight stitch or a narrow zigzag stitch, sew up the side with a quick seam, backstitching at the beginning and end. I sew the seam with a ½-inch (1.3 cm) seam allowance so I have room to square up and pink the seams after sewing. Using neon thread creates a bold contrast. You can also use a coordinating thread and let the stitches disappear into the fabric.

*Note: If you want to add a loop or tab, create a loop with a few inches of ribbon or cording and trap the ends into the side seam as you sew.*

## STEP 7

A quick pink with your shears squares everything up and gives a finished, decorative edge.

# MARBLED-TOED SHOES

Dip a scuff-toed shoe into a swirling pattern of color for an instant refresh.
This is a great project for shoes that have scuffs and stains from lots of wear.

## MATERIALS

Pair of faux leather flats or other
smooth shoes

Nail polish in preferred color palette

Large bowl of water

Bamboo skewer

Acetone and paper towels for cleanup

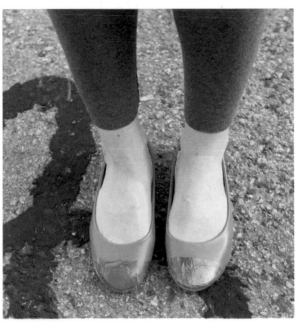

### STEP 1

Float several drops of nail polish on the surface of the water. Working quickly, swirl a design into the polish using a bamboo skewer.

### STEP 2

Holding the shoe straight up and down, dip the toe of the shoe directly into the water, and then pull it straight up.

### STEP 3

Repeat steps 1 and 2 on the other shoe and allow the shoes to dry on a paper towel for about 15 minutes, or until the polish is no longer tacky. Clean up the remaining polish with a paper towel. Remove any polish on the bowl with acetone, and then wash with soap and water.

### TROUBLESHOOTING

If you wait too long to dip your shoe, the floating polish can form a stiff skin that won't cling to the shoe well. If this happens, it's better to clean the surface of the water with a paper towel and start fresh.

If polishes don't react well together, try using all the same brand of nail polish.

*Note: If your shoes will get a lot of wear you may want to seal the polish with a clear spray varnish. Simply tape off the tip of the shoe with painter's tape just above the dip line, and spray the toe to seal.*

*Play with various color combinations and shoe colors for more subtle or striking results. Higher contrast color combinations will be bolder.*

# taking surface design
# to new dimensions

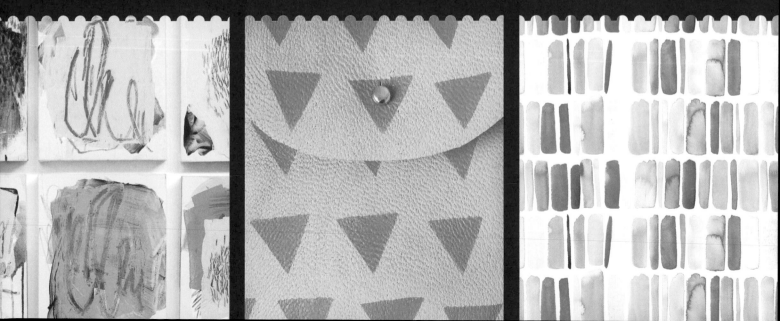

# JEN HEWETT

www.jenhewett.com

I love Jen Hewett's use of color and the way she combines simple shapes for impactful designs. Patches of coral, mustard, and black printed on natural gray linen look like marks left by a painter and placed asymmetrically on a classic clutch. Jen uses single lines over and over, splatters of paint, and dots and circles to create movement on each of her pieces. These marks are simple on their own, but create dynamic patterns when placed together.

Jen Hewett is a self-taught, San Francisco–based printmaker and surface designer. Working out of her tiny (54-square foot! [5 sq. m]) studio, Jen screen prints her bright, colorful work onto fabric, and then sews it into bags and pillows. Stores throughout the United States carry her bags, and her products have made their way to destinations all over the world. Except for a six-month stint in Paris, Jen has lived in California her entire life. She has a degree in English from the University of California, Berkeley.

*Triangles clutch*

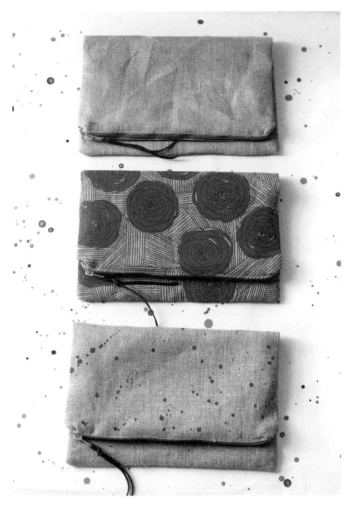

*Spring line*

*Disco dots tote*

*Pink-gold colorway*

*Roses clutch*

# LISA CONGDON

www.lisacongdon.com

Lisa Congdon is known for her simple line work and geometric shapes. Her use of stark black and white, paired with primary colors and offset with neons, creates her signature look. Recently, Lisa started sharing her more abstract approach to painting in addition to her graphic style of drawing. Her paintings are full of rich color patches that float in and out of focus, almost edible orbs of color that form dreamy backgrounds primed for black line work and structured shapes.

Her drawings and paintings translate beautifully into surface designs on goods such as linens, wallpaper, notebooks, and even apparel. I find it so inspiring to see Lisa's approach to painting and drawing. By taking a single, tiny shape and drawing it over and over, she creates a dazzling repeating pattern. Since 2007, she has been illustrating for clients including The Museum of Modern Art, *Martha Stewart Living* magazine, Chronicle Books, and Simon & Schuster, among many others. She has licensed her work for fabric, kitchen linens, wallpaper, bedding, and stationery. Her fine art work has been shown at such prestigious institutions as Bedford Gallery/Lesher Center for the Arts and the Contemporary Jewish Museum in San Francisco. In addition to painting and drawing full time, Lisa writes a popular daily blog of her work, life, and inspiration called *Today Is Going to Be Awesome*. She is the author of *Whatever You Are, Be a Good One* and *Art Inc.*

*Portal from the revelry fabric collection*

*From the Light*

*In the Heat of the Night*

*Tornado*

*Ghost Mountain*

*Stillness*

# PEGGY WOLF – BLACKBIRD AND THE OWL

www.peggywolf.com, www.blackbirdandtheowl.etsy.com

Peggy Wolf's use of simple motifs combined with the clean shapes of her leather goods make for a stunning combination.

Peggy Wolf is an illustrator turned designer with the birth of her company, Blackbird and the Owl. Peggy's main focus is creating bags that are minimal in their look and feel, yet have strong and clear design elements. Each piece of leather is screen printed with simple motifs in her studio and made into coin purses, clutches, and other accessories.

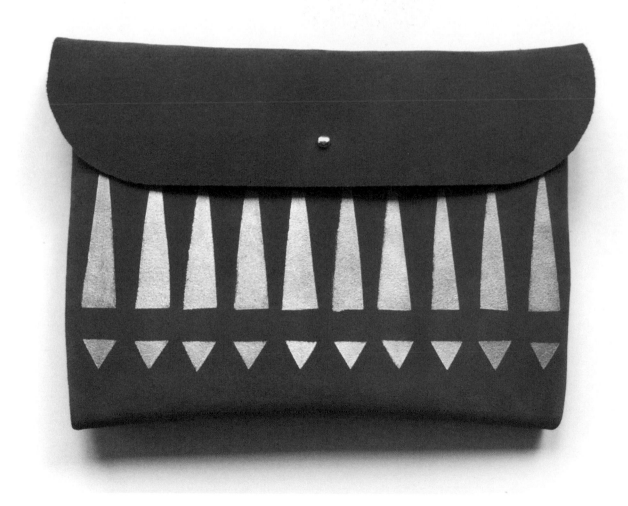

*Hand silk-screened leather accessories*

# JODY ALEXANDER

www.jalexbooks.com, www.wishiwashistudio.com

I fell in love with Jody Alexander's books first. Then, I was captivated by her characters and the environments she created for them. Now, I am calmed by her stitches and stamping, and the quiet way she approaches each piece. Jody's work moved and shifted over the years, but her attention to detail is unwavering. She incorporates repetitive marks made with thread, graphite, and geometric shapes stamped over and over to create dimension. In addition to its beauty, her work speaks to the deep level of thought and commitment she gives to each piece.

Jody Alexander is an artist, a bookbinder, a librarian, and a teacher who lives and works in Santa Cruz, California. She binds books with found and discarded papers and fabric in a number of historical and modern binding styles. She combines these books with found objects to create sculptural works. Her pieces celebrate collecting, story-telling, and odd characters. She also likes to rescue discarded books and give them new life as scrolls, wall pieces, and sculptural objects. Her characters, books, sculptural pieces, and found items are often combined to create installations.

*Max: Sans VIII*

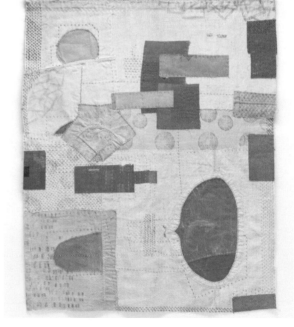

*Essential*

*KEEP Table Runner*

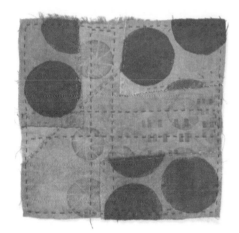

*KEEP Tabletop Cloth*

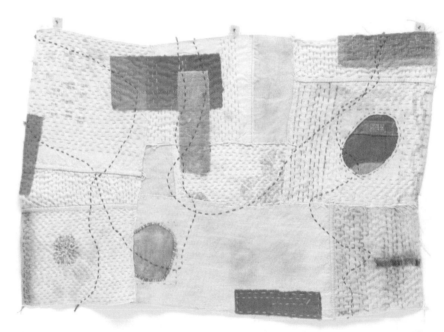

*Shakerag Hollow*

# YAO CHENG

www.yaochengdesign.com

Yao Cheng's works ranges from a repetition of
strokes on a page to beautifully rendered bouquets of
flowers—and everything in between. Most of her work
allows the medium of watercolor to move and play
throughout the image, adding a layer of beauty that
is so recognizably hers. I love how fresh her painting
style is no matter the subject!

*Spring Floral in turquoise*

*Blue Waves*

*Spring Melody*

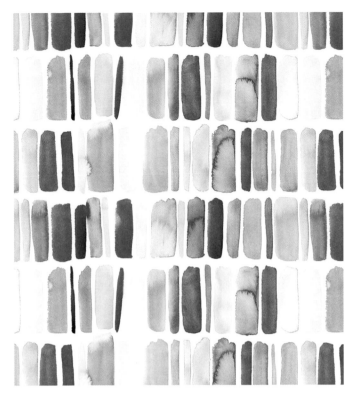

*Blue and turquoise rectangles*

*Blue Stripes*

*Triangle Melody*

*Blue triangles and dots*

# LARI WASHBURN

www.lariwashburn.com

I'm smitten with everything Lari does. From her paintings to ceramics to even a scrap of paper tucked in a sketchbook, her way of mark making entrances me.

Lari says, "I focus primarily on surface quality, particularly line quality and pattern. I want my work to captivate and refresh people purely through a visual experience, without involving the intellect. I'm interested in making a beautiful object when I make my art. I think this is in response to how demanding the world is of us, in terms of thinking, coping, and making meaning out of everything. I'd like my work to provide a little relief from that. I make paintings and drawings in mixed media, including acrylic, collage, and watercolor. I am also a textile designer."

*Sketchbook entry*

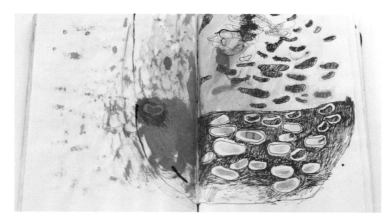

*Sketchbook entry*

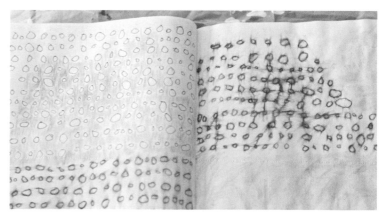

*Sketchbook entry*

*Stripe dot bowl*

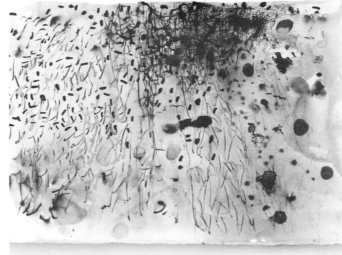

*Downpour*

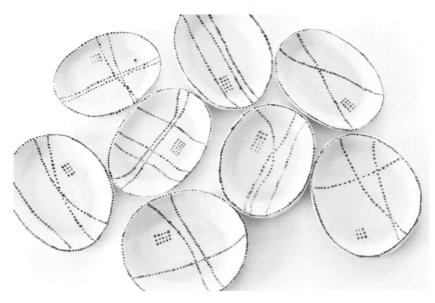

*Little appetizer plates*

# JODIE HURT

www.jodiehurt.com

Jodie Hurt and I met on Flickr many years ago by trading Artist Trading Cards (ATCs). I was instantly struck by Jodie's use of color in her collages and mixed-media pieces. Many years later, Jodie and I still trade work. Her monoprints, paintings, and general "play" are always bright, bold, and uplifting. Seeing her work on social media always inspires me to break out the paints and make something.

Jodie Hurt is a middle school art educator living in Kansas City, Kansas, who spends her free time playing with paper and paint. She loves combining fresh, bright colors and patterns with crumbling vintage textbook pages and reproductions of Victorian woodcut engravings. She also dabbles a bit in bookbinding, printmaking, and various forms of digital and analog photography.

*Ink drawing on paper*

*Monoprint*

*Monoprint*

*Monoprint*

*Monoprint*

*Monoprint*

*Mixed-media collage*

*Mixed-media collage*

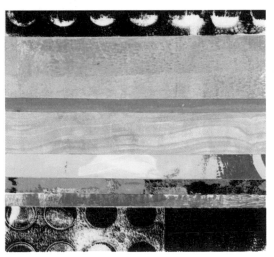

*Mixed-media collage*

# ANIKA STARMER

www.aisforanika.com

I first discovered Anika Starmer's work through Instagram and a shared love of drawing on index cards. Anika is fearless in her approach to pattern making. Armed with a few markers, pens, or paints, she can make a pattern of any mark or gesture. So inspiring!

Anika creates something new every day. When working on quick sketches or a finished piece of art, she uses a variety of materials, which is central to her process and explorations. She is always amazed by how changing from marker to a paintbrush or pastels to pencil can significantly change her approach to making art and lead her down new creative paths. Patterns and textures are the most common themes that Anika explores, although you can often find her sketching from life, especially after a walk in nature, during which she is sure to gather a few interesting finds, such as leaves, shells, or feathers. Nature has a way of integrating into Anika's pattern and surface design work, whether she is developing stylized motifs or incorporating organic textures and shapes into her abstract pieces. Her other love is color: bold and sometimes unexpected, it provides a contrast to natural themes. Anika is a freelance designer and artist living in Maryland with her two dachshund studio assistants, Otto and Kasi.

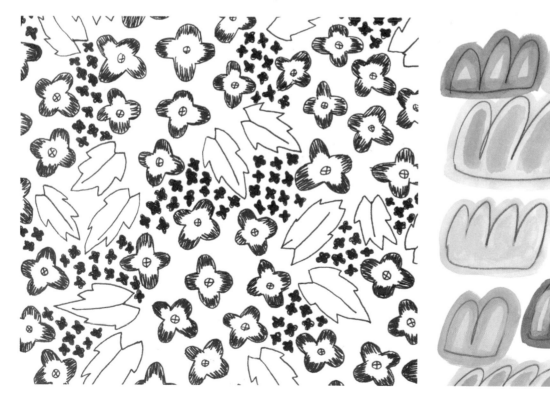

*Ink garden*

*Summer Hills*

*Day 42*

*Reef*

*Meadow*

*Loose dots*

# TYLER ROBBINS

www.shapeandcolor.bigcartel.com/artist/tyler-robbins

I discovered Tyler Robbins's work on Instagram. His handle is ShapeAndColor, and yet everything I saw (at first) was black and white. What I love most about Tyler's work is the movement of his strokes and the quality of his line work. Simple shapes dance and move to create forms, patterns, and even vibrations.

Tyler says, "I find the most honest and exciting ideas lay beneath critical thought. Drawing, painting, or creating anything with impatient urgency allows ideas to evolve before they're corrupted by reason."

*Sockeye*

*Collective Understanding (detail)*

*Birdsnake*

*Monument Falls*

*The Hunt Turns*

# HEATHER DAY

www.heatherdayart.com

It took me a while to come around to abstract painting, but had I met Heather Day earlier I might have changed my mind about it long ago. The colors, marks, and gestures in Heather's paintings seem effortless. I love her use of color, and the way she balances large patches of paint with small obsessive marks and wide slashes and scribbles. Best of all, her work feels fun even in its seriousness.

Heather Day was born in Ewa Beach, Hawaii, and spent her younger years living in Washington, DC. She received her BFA in painting and art history from Maryland Institute College of Art (MICA) in Baltimore. Heather currently lives in San Francisco and paints in her Oakland studio. Her work involves a process of layering paint and experimenting with various techniques of mark making.

*The Things You Told Me Today,* PHOTO: KATHRYN RUMMEL

*We Were Sleeping, Birthday*

*Portraits of You*

*We Were Sleeping, Birthday*

*We Were Sleeping, #4*

# ALEXANDRA JEAN

www.ajeanstudio.com

Alexandra Jean's bold graphic patterns and sophisticated color palette are what drew me to her work. I love her constant exploration into what she prints and how she develops patterns.

Alexandra Jean is a multidisciplinary freelance graphic designer based in Brussels. Her activities are textile design and visual communication. Her printing workshop is an exploratory field that allows her to develop research, motifs, and color ranges for application in architecture, design, and fashion. As a member of the group "110 par minute" Alexandra Jean also aims to improve the knowledge of the art of textile design through exhibitions, performances, and exclusive sales.

*Anasstasia, print series 1*          *Gaetane, print series 1*          *Hortense, print series 1*

*Elisabelle, print series 1, 2 & 3*

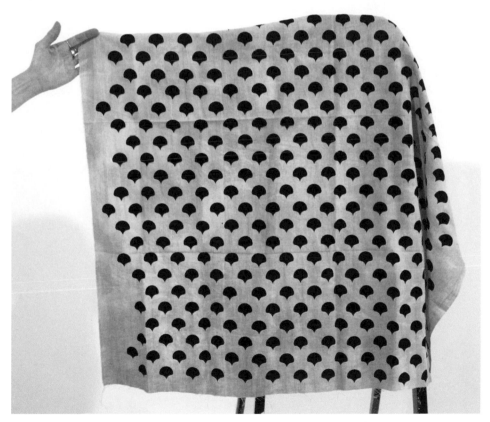

*Abbygaelle, print series 1*

*Franceline, print series 1, 2 & 3*

*Franceline, print series 4*

# BIRCH & GOLDBERRY

www.etsy.com/shop/BirchandGoldberry

Enchanted by the subtleties of the natural world, Birch & Goldberry create a festive collective of paper products, including greeting cards and hand-painted wrapping paper as well as a variety of petite presents, such as soy candles and handcrafted soaps.

*Assortment of hand-painted gift wrap*

# RESOURCES

**Arch**
www.archsupplies.com
One of my favorite, local art supplies stores, Arch has a little bit of everything and then some.

**Blick Art Supply**
www.dickblick.com
Acrylic paints, fabric and textile paints, brushes, and wood panels.

**Creativebug**
www.creativebug.com
Online video workshop resource with classes from top designers and artists across all categories. You can find classes with Courtney Cerruti as well as other artists, in addition to crafting resources and inspiration.

**Dharma Trading Co.**
www.dharmatrading.com
For textiles, paints, blank totes, and other linens.

**Flax**
www.flaxart.com
Another local favorite, as well as a San Francisco staple, Flax has an entire room full of flat files that house fine art papers in addition to paints, brushes, and more.

**Michaels**
www.michaels.com
A good place to source a variety of basic art and craft supplies.

**Paper Source**
www.papersource.com
I love the text-weight paper from Paper Source. It's heavier than most text papers, making it perfect for paste paper and collage, plus it comes in a beautiful range of colors. You can also find methyl cellulose in small quantities here, as well as a number of other art and craft goodies.

**Purl Soho**
www.purlsoho.com
Both the brick-and-mortar and the online store are a feast for the eyes. Purl has a beautifully curated collection of fabrics, wool, yarn, and other sewing and crafting supplies. I LOVE the wool felt for the keepsake pouches project, as well as their selection of tapestry wool for the marble tassels project. Purl also has amazing trims for tying up packages and gifts!

**SEO Studio**
www.saraheowen.com
The studio of Sarah E. Owen, where we did one of the shoots for this book.

**Tallas Book Binding Supply**
www.talasonline.com
This bookbinder's supply has most traditional materials for bookbinding and restoration. You can find large quantities of methyl cellulose and other marbling supplies.

**TaTa Indian Wooden Stamps**
www.etsy.com/shop/
TATAindianwoodstamps
Amazing selection of wooden stamps for printing on paper and fabric. I love the variety of motifs from traditional to modern.

# ABOUT THE AUTHOR

Maker extraordinaire, Courtney Cerruti is an artist and the author of *Playing with Image Transfers: Exploring Creative Imagery for Use in Art, Mixed Media, and Design* and *Washi Tape: 101+ Ideas for Paper Crafts, Book Arts, Fashion, Decorating, Entertaining, and Party Fun!* She teaches workshops at the San Francisco Center for the Book, Makeshift Society, and online at Creativebug.com. She is addicted to Instagram (@ccerruti), washi tape, and all things old and worn. She lives in the San Francisco Bay Area in a tiny space with her pup, Charlie, where she is surrounded by paintings, beautiful objects, and myriad collections.

Use the hashtag #PlayingWithSurfaceDesign when posting your projects on social media. Feel free to tag at @ccerruti. I'd love to see what you make!

# ACKNOWLEDGMENTS

Many thanks to my friends and family who always support me—for being cheerleaders when I need them; for listening; and for offering words of encouragement at the best and the worst of times—I love you all.

Thank you, Liz, for working on this book with me. You are a generous and kind spirit, who was patient even when pup Charlie peed on your rug!!! I love working with you! XO

Many thanks to Sarah, for letting us shoot photos in your stunning space! Special thanks to Jonathan Simcosky for coaching and guiding me along the way—I needed every bit of it! Thanks to the folks at Quarry for working on this project and seeing it all the way through to the final book. Thank you to all my students. I am a better teacher because of you, and I am so grateful.

XO
Courtney